Charles Darwin

Naturalist

GREAT MINDS OF SCIENCE

Charles Darwin
Naturalist

Margaret J. Anderson

ENSLOW PUBLISHERS, INC.

Bloy St. & Ramsey Ave.	P.O. Box 38
Box 777	Aldershot
Hillside, N.J. 07205	Hants GU12 6BP
U.S.A.	U.K.

To John A. Hall
Naturalist

Library of Congress Cataloging-In-Publication Data

Anderson, Margaret Jean, 1931-
    Charles Darwin, naturalist / Margaret J. Anderson.
        p. cm. — (Great minds of science)
    Includes bibliographical references and index.
    ISBN 0-89490-476-0
    1. Darwin, Charles, 1809–1882—Juvenile literature.
    2. Naturalists—England—Biography—Juvenile literature.
    [1. Darwin, Charles, 1809-1882. 2. Naturalists.] I. Title. II. Series.
    QH31. D2A785 1994
    575'.0092—dc20
    [B]   93-29839
                                                                    CIP
                                                                    AC
Printed in the United States

10 9 8 7 6 5 4 3 2 1

Illustration Credit: Kim Austin, pp. 12, 40–41, 46, 58, 91; Margaret J. Anderson, pp. 73, 104, 114; Gretchen Bracher, pp. 8, 23; Cambridge University Museum of Archaeology and Anthropology, p. 48; Frances Chapple, pp. 29, 30; Photo by M.A. Houck, pp. 31, 87, 110; Photos by P. Komar, pp. 67, 77, 81, 92, 101, 107, 109, 117; By courtesy of James Moore, pp. 19, 69; National Maritime Museum, London, p. 38; Photo from "Journal of Reseaches. . ." 1871, Appleton and Co., Courtesy of Alison and Andrew Moldenke, p. 74; Gordon Pritchard, 59, 60, 61; The Wellcome Institute Library, London, pp. 10, 35, 84.

Cover Photo Credits: Mauricio Handler/The Wildlife Collection (background); P. Komar (inset).

Contents

Famous Birthday

THE DARWIN FAMILY LIVED IN A SMALL, country town in the west of England. Their house was named The Mount. It was a solid, red-brick house on a hill above the River Severn. Robert Darwin was a doctor. He stood six-feet, two-inches tall and was heavyset. He weighed more than 300 pounds. He looked as solid and important as his house.

Dr. Darwin was well liked by his patients. They told him their family problems as well as their medical problems. He wasn't always so well liked at home. He had a habit of giving two-hour-long lectures. No one was allowed to interrupt.

Susannah Darwin did not have as much to say as her husband did. She was a quiet woman. She ran the house and kept track of the family budget. Her good business sense came from her father. When her father was a young man, he had started

The home of the Darwin family—The Mount.

up a pottery works. His name was Josiah Wedgwood. Wedgwood china is famous to this day.

Susannah's father died the year before she was married. He left the pottery business to his son. He left his daughter £25,000. With Susannah's money and the doctor's practice, the Darwins could afford a big house.

Charles Robert Darwin was their fifth child. He was born on February 12, 1809. He was named Charles after an uncle. Uncle Charles had died young while he was studying to become a doctor. Doctors ran in the Darwin family. Charles's grandfather had been a doctor, too. Robert was hoping that his new son would follow in their footsteps. No one could have guessed that the tiny baby was not going to be a doctor, but one of the most famous scientists of all time. His ideas would change the world.

When Charles grew older, he went off to school. His family and his teachers still had no idea that they were bringing up a genius. He struck them as a quiet, plodding boy. Yet even then Charles was getting ready for his place in history as a naturalist

Charles Darwin's father, Dr. Robert Darwin (1766-1848).

and a thinker. He loved to collect things. He collected shells, coins, rocks, insects, and birds' eggs. He knew the names of flowers and beetles. He liked to take long walks by himself.

Young Charles's most important lessons were not learned in the classroom.

Charles Darwin shared his birth date with another baby whose ideas would shape the world. This other baby was not born in a big house. His home was a log cabin in Kentucky. His name was Abraham Lincoln. Young Abraham's school days were few. But his thirst for learning was great. He read the family Bible over and over again. He also read any other books he could get his hands on. In 1861, just before he turned fifty-two, Lincoln became the sixteenth president of the United States. It was a stormy time to be president. He led his nation through a civil war.

Charles Darwin, on the other hand, almost *caused* a civil war. He wrote a book called *The Origin of Species*. The book was published in England in 1859. That was two years before Lincoln became president of the United States. Darwin's book led

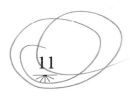

After his 5-year trip around the world, Charles never left Britain again.

to an angry debate between scientists and church leaders in Britain. Some people were both scientists and church leaders. *The Origin of Species* raised troubling questions.

What was this new idea that upset people so much?

Darwin's book explained how new kinds, or species, of plants and animals get started. His book is about *evolution*. Evolution means "a slow change or unfolding." Charles claimed that over time small differences among similar plants or animals can give rise to new species. He said that this is still going on. New species are still forming.

The Origin of Species upset some people because it appeared to go against the Bible. The first book of the Bible describes how God made the world in seven days. He made all the kinds of plants and animals. He made man and woman. Charles was saying that not all plants and animals were created at the same time. Also, for his theory to be true, the world would need to be far older than most people thought.

Scientists who named plants and animals did

not like this new idea either. They said that species were fixed. They could not change.

Darwin was not the first person to come up with the idea of evolution. It had been around long before his book came out. Geologists—people who study the earth—had noticed that the landscape changes with time. Some changes are sudden; others are slow. Earthquakes and volcanoes can make mountains. Wind and rain wear away rocks. Slow changes take place over millions of years.

Charles's own grandfather had written a book about changes in plants and animals.[1] Charles, however, took the idea further. He had noticed that some groups of birds are more closely related to each other than to other birds. He pictured them on the same main branch of a family tree. They had a common ancestor. He went on to explain how new kinds of plants or animals could begin.

Many of Darwin's examples came from things he collected on a trip around the world. He was a naturalist on a sailing ship called the *Beagle*. People in Britain were interested in the flowers and animals of the new world. Museums wanted new plants, birds, and insects for their collections.

The *Beagle*'s main job, however, was not to look for new plants and animals. It was to chart the coastline of South America. While the crew was busy taking readings and making maps, Charles was free to go on shore. He did more than just collect. He took careful notes. He also did a lot of thinking. He was amazed by the wide range of plants and animals he saw. He wondered why there were so many different kinds. He thought about ways in which animals living now are like those we only know from fossils. The result of all this thinking was *The Origin of Species*.

Most scientists who come up with an exciting new idea can't wait to write it up. While they are working on it, they are forever looking over their shoulders. They worry that someone else might stumble on their idea and get it into print first. Not so for Darwin. Twenty-three years passed after the *Beagle* returned to England before *The Origin of Species* was published. It was, in the end, another scientist coming up with the same theory that forced Darwin into print. Otherwise, he would have put it off longer.

Whole books have been written on why Darwin did not want to share his ideas with the world. Darwin, the man, is almost as interesting a study as his theory of evolution. When he was old, Charles Darwin wrote his own life story.[2] He wrote it for his children and grandchildren. It is quite a short book of around 150 pages. Since then, many people have written Darwin's life story. Some of their books are up to 700 pages. Darwin—who was a modest man—would be surprised to find himself the object of so much thought. On the other hand, he might not be so surprised. Deep thinking was his specialty.

School Days

WHEN CHARLES WAS YOUNG, THERE WERE
no telephones. People kept in touch by writing
long letters. Each week, Mrs. Darwin wrote to her
brother, Jos. Jos and his family lived about thirty
miles away in the village of Maer. Their mansion
was called Maer Hall. We know a lot about the
Darwins from Susannah's letters. They were about
everyday matters—the weather, family visits, and,
of course, her children.

When Charles was just over a year old, Mrs.
Darwin had her sixth child. The baby was a girl.
They named her Catherine. The oldest three
children were also girls. Marianne was twelve,

Caroline was nine, and Susan was six. Then came five-year-old Erasmus. He was named for his grandfather, but he was mostly called Ras.

The children were often sick. Their mother spent long hours by their bedsides. Back then, there were no shots or antibiotics. A child could die from an illness that would not be serious now. Even though there was a doctor in the house, Mrs. Darwin was not free from worry. Sometimes, it seemed to add to the worry. In one letter, she told Jos that Dr. Darwin was spending the night in a house where four children and a servant were very sick. They had scarlet fever. Mrs. Darwin was afraid that the doctor might bring the sickness home.

Mrs. Darwin herself had poor health. She had not been well since the birth of her second child. By the time Charles was born, the older girls did most of the work. When he was a small boy, Charles thought his teenage sisters were far too bossy. Marianne did the housework. Caroline's job was to teach the two youngest ones—Charles and Catherine. Catherine was smart and learned her

Young Charles Darwin with sister Catherine.

lessons quickly. Charles was mischievous. Caroline
was always scolding him. Whenever he went into
a room where his sister was, he used to ask himself,
"What will she blame me for now?"[1]

And young Charles was not blameless!

He sometimes told fibs in order to get the
others to notice him. His fibs were often about
strange birds or animals he said he had seen on
his walks. He felt badly afterwards. Once, to cause

a bit of excitement, Charles picked some peaches and plums from the trees in the garden. He hid the fruit in the bushes. Then he rushed into the house to spread the news that he had found a hoard of stolen fruit!

Most of the naughty things that Charles did as a child were tied in with his interest in nature. He told a boy at school that he could make primroses different colors by watering them with different-colored liquids. Another time, he said that his mother had taught him to find out a plant's name by looking inside the blossom.

Charles's sisters did not like him to collect birds' eggs. They made a rule that he must never take more than one egg from a nest. One time he took all the eggs. He didn't really want them all. He was just rebelling against his sisters. But mostly he did what they said. While the family was on vacation on the Welsh coast, Charles found some new insects. Of course, he wanted to collect them. The girls told him it was cruel to kill insects. They would only let him take ones that were already dead. So he didn't end up with much of a collection. Fishing was another of Charles's favorite hobbies. The older girls could not stand the idea of a live, wiggling worm on a hook. Charles had to kill the worms in salt water before baiting the hook. That meant he didn't catch as many fish, but he always did it their way.

Mrs. Darwin died when Charles was eight and one-half years old. Later, he wrote that all he could remember about his mother was "her deathbed, her black velvet gown, and her curiously constructed work table."[2] Even though he could remember other things about his early life, he had only those few memories of his mother. The girls did not talk about her after she died. The Darwins kept their feelings to themselves.

Dr. Darwin did not talk about his grief, either. He grew moody and spent more time than ever with his patients. When he was at home, he was not easy to be around. The young children were rather afraid of him. He was such a big man, and he had such a sharp tongue. Luckily, there were visits to Maer Hall to look forward to. The children often rode over there to spend time with Uncle

Jos, Aunt Bessie, and the Wedgwood cousins—all eight of them.

The Wedgwood children did not like the return visits to The Mount. One of the older cousins wrote to an aunt about a visit to the Darwins' house. They spent the afternoon waiting for Dr. Darwin to come home. He was out seeing his patients. In her letter, she said, "Sunday we dined about half-past-one, drest afterwards, and sat about 3 hours expecting the tide to come in about dark, and rather stiff and awful the evening was."[3]

When Charles was nine, he was sent off to a boarding school. Ras was already a student there. The school was only about a mile away. Charles often ran home in the evening, but he had to get back to school before lock-up time—the time each night when the doors were locked. Locked doors were not the only way in which the school was like a prison. The boys slept in a long, cold, gloomy room. They had one blanket each. Meals were skimpy. The water for bathing was cold. Dr. Butler, the headmaster, was very strict. He drilled his students in Latin, Greek, and ancient history.

These were subjects that Charles had no use for. He was only an average student. It was a struggle for him to learn long passages of Latin verse.

If science had been taught in schools back then, Charles's talent might have been noticed earlier. He did get a chance to learn chemistry. Ras had set up a lab in a toolshed in the garden at The Mount. He let Charles help him with some of the

A sketch of Shrewsbury School, where Charles first attended classes.

experiments. When the boys at school heard about this, they nicknamed Charles "Gas." Even Dr. Butler got wind of it. He scolded Charles for wasting his time on useless subjects.

Often Charles escaped the boredom of his lessons by losing himself in a book. He spent hours reading the plays of Shakespeare. His hideaway was an old window seat set into the thick walls of the school.

In the summer, he learned to shoot. Suddenly he had a new passion. He was so excited when he shot his first snipe that he could scarcely reload his gun. Maer Hall, with its woods and its lake, was now more of a magnet than ever.

Charles's schooldays ended when he was sixteen. Dr. Darwin was beginning to worry that his younger son cared for "nothing but shooting, dogs, and rat catching."[4] He was afraid that the boy would be a disgrace to himself and the family. He told Charles that it was time for him to get serious about a career. Charles was sent off to Edinburgh University in Scotland. He was to follow in the family footsteps and become a doctor.

In Search of a Career

CHARLES DID NOT GO TO SCOTLAND alone. Brother Ras went too. Ras was also going to be a doctor. He had done his course work in England. By doing his hospital work in Edinburgh, the brothers could be together.

After Charles and Ras had found a place to stay, they set off to explore the city. Between the new part of the town and the old town was a deep ravine. A busy street ran along it. On the way up to the university, the brothers crossed a bridge over this street. In a letter home, Charles wrote: "When we first looked over the side, we could hardly believe our eyes. Instead of a fine river we saw streams of people."[1] They could also see an old castle. It perched on a huge rock high above the city.

Dr. Darwin had many friends in Edinburgh. These friends invited the Darwin sons to their homes. They took them to the theater and to meetings. They took them to concerts. Charles met several famous people. One was Sir Walter Scott. Charles had read some of his books. Another was John Audubon, who gave a talk on American birds.

But Charles had gone to Edinburgh to study. And that was not going so well. He found lectures dull. He would rather learn from books than listen to lectures. He did not want to hear Dr. Duncan talk about the healing ways of plants. He did not care to know what rhubarb was good for—especially not at eight o'clock on a raw winter morning.

Worse than lectures was having to watch operations. Charles saw only two. Both times he ran from the room before the operation was over. One was on a child. This was before painkillers were used. Charles could not bear the sight of blood or the sound of the screams.

Later on, Charles wished he had spent more time in his anatomy class. But he did pick up one new skill that first year. He learned to stuff birds. He was taught by a freed black slave named John Edmonstone. John lived on the same street as Charles. He worked in the city museum. While Charles learned to stuff birds, John told him about his life as a slave in South America. He also told him about the rain forests there. Charles had no idea that one day he would see these forests for himself.

Charles was glad when his first year of college was over. Summer was more fun. He went hiking in Wales. He kept a diary. In it he wrote about all the birds and animals he saw. When August came, he put away his diary and got out his gun. Hunting was still his passion.

When it was time to go back to Edinburgh, he went alone. Ras was through with his studies. Charles made new friends. Many of them were scientists. One was Dr. Robert Grant. Grant was almost twice as old as Charles. The two of them used to go for long walks along the coast. Grant knew a lot about sea creatures. He was interested in sponges. Were they animals or plants? He thought they must be a primitive, or early, form of life. Charles began to learn about marine life too.

Charles's letters home were all about his friends. He told about going out on a fishing boat. He checked the fishermen's nets for new sea animals. He had given a talk at science meetings on one of his finds. He didn't say much about his classes. Dr. Darwin could tell that Charles was not going to follow in his footsteps after all. Maybe his son should study for the church instead. He didn't want him to be a good-for-nothing.

Charles was not sure that he wanted to be a minister. But then he thought about it some more. He wouldn't need to spend all his time writing sermons. If he had a country church, he could study nature. Besides, that was still three years away. He had to get a degree first. So he went to Cambridge University in England.

Unsure of his future, Charles attended Christ's College of Cambridge University.

Years later, Charles wrote that his time at Cambridge was the most joyful and happy in his life. He was in good health and almost always in high spirits. But once again, he found lectures dull. And again, he made lots of friends. He took up new hobbies. One of these was really an old hobby—looking for beetles. Collecting beetles was what everyone was doing. Charles was one of the best collectors. One day, when he tore off some bark from a tree, he saw two rare beetles. Then he saw a third—a new kind. He didn't have a hand free to catch it, so he popped the beetle in his right hand into his mouth. The beetle gave off a bad tasting fluid. Charles spat the beetle out and lost it. He lost the new one as well.

In 1964, Cambridge University opened a new college named in honor of the Darwin family.

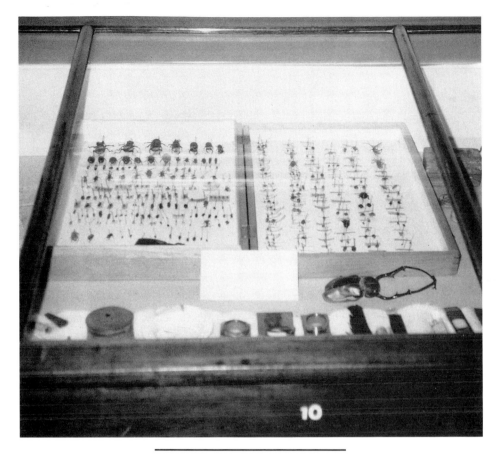

Charles's cousin William Darwin Fox inspired him to begin his lifelong study of beetles.

Latin and Greek were as dull as ever. There were, however, some teachers Charles liked. They just didn't teach the classes he had to take. One was Professor Henslow. He taught botany, the study of plants. Charles went along on field trips.

Looking for plants was almost as much fun as looking for beetles. One time he saw a rare, insect-eating plant in a bog on the other side of a ditch. He tried to pole vault across. The pole stuck in the mud, straight up, with Charles on top. Feeling foolish, he slid down into the mud. But he did get the rare plant. Charles stood out as a keen collector. Something else that Henslow noticed—and liked—about Charles was that he was curious. He asked a lot of questions.

Another teacher Charles admired was Professor Sedgwick. He taught geology, the study of the landscape and rocks. After his final exams, Charles went on a tour of North Wales with Professor Sedgwick. It was a one-on-one course in geology. Charles learned far more on that trip than he could ever have learned from books. He found two old bones in a cave. The land owner had found a rhinoceros tooth in these same caves. Charles was amazed at the thought that rhinos had once wandered over the Welsh hills.

But now summer was over. It was time to think

about finding a job. But first, Charles planned to go to Maer Hall to hunt birds. He stopped in at home on the way to Maer Hall. There was a letter waiting for him. It was from Professor Henslow. Charles didn't know it then, but this letter would change his life.

The Great Adventure

THE LETTER FROM HENSLOW WAS ABOUT a job. The job was not in the church, but as a naturalist. And it was not in England. It was on board a sailing ship called the *Beagle*. The captain of the *Beagle* was named Robert FitzRoy. He was a young man, twenty-six years old. He was going to map the coast of South America. He figured the trip would take two years. As captain of the ship, he could not mix with the crew. He wanted someone to go along as a friend. This friend would share his cabin and his dinner table. He was also to study the natural history of places where they stopped.

FitzRoy's first choice had been Henslow himself. But Mrs. Henslow did not want her husband to be gone that long. So Henslow told FitzRoy about Charles Darwin. Charles made friends easily. He was keen on nature. He had just been on a trip to learn all about rocks and the landscape. He was a skillful rider and hunter. And he was young—just twenty-two years old.

Robert FitzRoy, captain of the Beagle. *In those days the captain never mixed with the crew. FitzRoy wanted someone to be his companion as well as to be the ship's naturalist.*

Charles thought the trip would be fun. However, his father saw things differently. This was not the time for his son to take off around the world. He should settle down. Besides, this was a job with no pay. He would need an allowance. Dr. Darwin said that Charles should say no. But he added, "If you can find any man of common sense, who advises you to go, I will give my consent."[1]

Sadly, Charles turned down the offer.

The next day, he set off for Maer to go hunting as planned. When he got there, he told Uncle Jos about the letter. Uncle Jos was all in favor of Charles going with FitzRoy. So instead of going out to hunt birds, the two of them rode back to The Mount. Charles had found a man of common sense who advised him to go. Dr. Darwin gave in.

Charles thanked his father. Then they talked about an allowance. Charles had sometimes run out of money while he was a student. He joked that he would have to be clever to spend more than his allowance while he was living on a boat.

"But they tell me you are very clever," Dr. Darwin answered with a smile.[2]

Charles hurried off to see Captain FitzRoy. He almost didn't get the job after all. FitzRoy thought he could tell a man's character from his face. He did not like the shape of Darwin's nose! But in the end, he decided to give him a chance.

The Origin of Species would not have been written if these two men—the doctor and the captain—had not changed their minds.

The *Beagle* sailed on December 27, 1831. They had no sooner left port than Charles became sick. He never did get used to the motion of the waves. There was a young man on board named Jemmy Button. He was on his way home to Tierra del Fuego at the tip of South America. When Charles was seasick, Jemmy tried to comfort him. He would lean over the hammock and say, "Poor, poor fellow!"[3]

The *Beagle*'s first stop was the Cape Verde Islands. They lie 300 miles west of the coast of Africa. The islands are mostly bare rock, but Charles was glad to be on solid ground. He found lots to look at. A white band ran through the dark rock about thirty feet up the side of a cliff. The band was made up of shells and coral. Did this mean that the land had once been under water? If so, how had it gotten to where it was now? Wherever he went, Charles was full of questions. Then he thought up possible answers.

On February 16, the *Beagle* crossed the equator. This was Charles's first time to be in the southern waters. The sailors were ready. They caught

The H.M.S Beagle's mission was to map the coastline of South America, and to study the natural history of the places they visited.

Charles and blindfolded him. Then they flipped him into a sail filled with water. Soon everyone on board was caught up in the water fight. Before it was over, even Captain FitzRoy was soaked.

On Leap Year's day in 1832, they reached Brazil. Charles went on shore and explored the forest. That night he wrote in his journal "such a day brings deeper pleasure than I could hope to find again."[4] He was amazed at the wild tangle of growth. He loved the sounds and the quietness. The drone of insects was so loud that it could be heard in a boat several hundred yards from shore. Yet in the deep forest, the silence was total.

The *Beagle* sailed on down the coast.

Just after midnight on the first of April, a man burst into the cabin. He asked Charles if he had ever seen a dolphin. Charles was out of his hammock like a shot. The night watch greeted him with shouts of laughter. It was an April Fool's joke.

The next stop was Rio de Janeiro, Brazil. Letters were waiting for Charles. They were full of news and gossip. All his friends seemed to be getting married. He felt very lonely at the thought

The Voyage
OF THE
Beagle

1. Dec. 27, 1831
   Sails from Plymouth,
   England

2. January 16, 1832
   Visits Cape Verde
   Islands

3. February 29, 1832
   Arrives in Brazil

4. Apr. - Dec. 1832
   Maps east coast
   of South America

5. December 17, 1832
   Arrives in Tierra
   del Fuego

6. 1833 - 1834
   Visits Falkland Islands
   Maps east coast
   of South America

7. February 1834
   Revisits Tierra
   del Fuego

8. June 10, 1834
   Sails into the
   Pacific Ocean

9. July 1834 - July 1835
   Maps west coast of
   South America

10. Sept. 16 - Oct. 20, 1835
    Visits Galapagos Islands

11. November 1835
    Visits Tahiti

12. March 1836
    Visits Southwest
    Australia

13. April 1836
    Visits Cocos (Keeling)
    Islands

14. October 2, 1836
    Returns to England

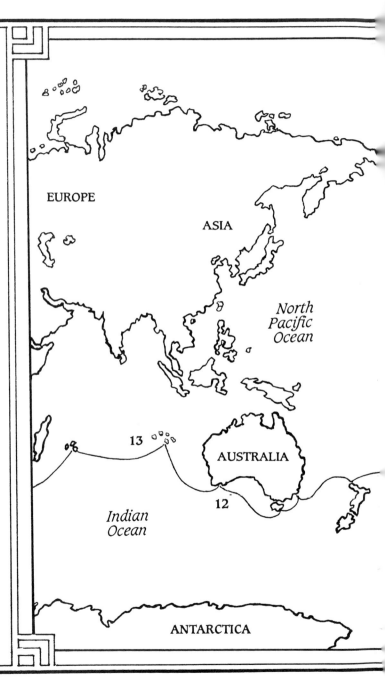

EUROPE

ASIA

North
Pacific
Ocean

AUSTRALIA

Indian
Ocean

ANTARCTICA

13

12

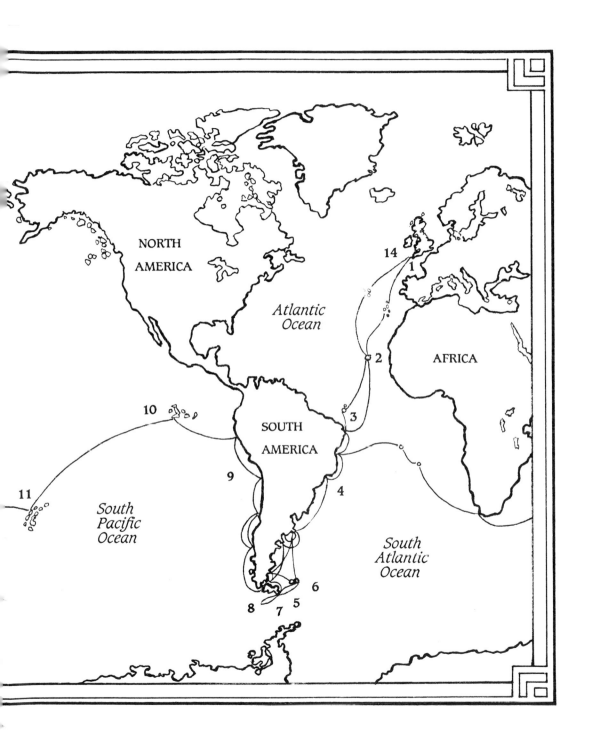

of the long trip ahead. Had he known the journey would take five years, he would have felt worse.

Charles threw himself into his work. He lived on shore for several weeks while the *Beagle* sailed north again. He rode up country to an estate where he saw slaves. He was very upset by the way their masters treated them. Back on the *Beagle*, he told FitzRoy that he thought all slaves should be freed. FitzRoy said that most slaves were happy with their lot. Charles began to argue, but FitzRoy lost his temper. So Charles learned to keep his thoughts to himself. There was still a long trip ahead. It was not a good idea to fight with the captain.

Farther south, Charles again saw trouble between different races of people. He was now in frontier country. Spanish settlers wanted to clear the plains of the native peoples. Gauchos, or cowboys, killed the natives with as little thought as they killed wild game. Even chiefs carrying white flags and wanting to talk peace were shot. Those were cruel and terrible days.

Charles rode through this "Devil's Country"

with the gauchos. He earned the respect of his rough companions. His hunting days back at Maer were paying off. He rode well. He could bring down game with his first shot. He ate roast armadillo. It tasted like duck.

Charles was eager to see every new kind of animal. The gauchos often hunted a fast-running bird called a rhea. They told Charles about another kind of rhea that was smaller and very rare. It was found farther south. Charles finally saw one. It was on his dinner plate! One of the crew had shot it and given it to the cook. The cook still had the head, legs, and one wing. Charles got them for his collection.

Riding with the gauchos was exciting. Finding fossils was even better. Charles came across the fossil leg bones of a giant sloth. They were from an extinct species. When Charles carried his find up the gang plank of the *Beagle*, he was teased about his cargo of rubbish. The next day, he went back to the same place. This time he found a large skull in some soft rock. By the time he was through, he also had teeth from a huge extinct rodent and giant armadillo shells. He packed the bones carefully. Then he sent them to Henslow on a boat that was bound for England.

The *Beagle* sailed still farther south. It was now December. This was summer in these southern waters, but the wind was as cold as winter back home. They had reached the coast of Tierra del Fuego. The steep, rocky hillsides were clothed in dark beech forests. Even in summer the leaves were drab and brown.

The weather turned wild. But it was not as wild as the people who lived in this harsh land. Charles was stunned by the sight of naked people yelling from the cliff tops. They had long, tangled hair and painted faces. He thought they looked like spirits from another world.

Land of Fire

FITZROY ORDERED THE CREW TO DROP anchor. Some of the men lowered a rowboat. They were going to land on Tierra del Fuego. Charles went with them. Up on the cliff, the wild men watched every move. As the small boat drew near the land, they scrambled down the rocks. They began to yell and wave their arms. They seemed to be showing the sailors where to pull in. But it was hard to be sure. They looked very fierce. Their copper-colored faces were streaked with white chalk and black mud.

The people of Tierra del Fuego were out-of-touch with the rest of the world. They were very different from Englishmen. Even though the climate was cold and wet, they did not build houses. Nor did they live in caves. The nearest thing to a shelter was a windbreak made of branches and grass. They slept huddled together on the bare ground. With no fixed homes, they wandered from place to place in search of food. They mostly ate mussels that they found on the rocks at low tide. When all the mussels in one area had been eaten, they moved on.

The Fuegians knew how to make rough boats from bark. They fished in the shallow waters of the bay. Sometimes they caught seals or otters, killing them with stones. The beaches were covered with big pebbles as smooth and round as oranges. The Fuegians used these stones for weapons when they fought nearby tribes.

Life was only possible in that cold, bleak land because the Fuegians knew how to make fire. They kept their fires going night and day. They even took fire along when they went fishing. They set live coals on a bed of sand in the middle of the canoe. As a sign of greeting or farewell, they piled green leaves on their fires to make columns of smoke. These smoke columns had given the land its name. Tierra del Fuego means "Land of Fire."

Charles found the Fuegians strange and interesting. He puzzled over how they came to live in that bleak land. What he wrote about them sometimes sounds unfeeling. This is partly due to the words he used. In his day, such people were often called savages. Charles wrote in his diary that he could not believe "how wide the difference

The natives of Tierra del Fuego led extremely simple lives compared to Charles Darwin's Europe. They wore little clothing, even in snow. They made windbreaks of grass and branches for shelter.

between savage and civilized man. It is greater than between a wild and domesticated animal."[1]

Some of his surprise was because he already knew three Fuegians. They were quite civilized. He had met them on the *Beagle*. One was Jemmy Button. The others were York Minster and Fuegia

Basket. Fuegia was a young girl. All three had been to school in England. They had learned English and farming. Now they were going home to teach the rest of their people these skills.

FitzRoy had thought up this plan. He had been to the Land of Fire three years earlier. While he was ashore, some Fuegians stole his rowboat. FitzRoy took four hostages, hoping to get the boat back. He tossed someone a pearl button from his coat in payment for Jemmy. That's how he got the name Jemmy Button.

The Fuegians did not bring the boat back.

So the *Beagle* sailed with the hostages on board. When they got to England, one of the Fuegians died. The other three were sent to school. They boarded with their teacher. FitzRoy paid all the fees. They settled down quite well. They liked wearing clothes. They liked the new kinds of food. Fuegia Basket was a good student. Jemmy made friends easily. He took great pride in how he looked. He loved to wear white gloves. He shined his shoes every day. York, the oldest, was always rather glum.

FirzRoy made sure that they were treated well. He even took them to London to meet the king. The queen gave Fuegia one of her own bonnets as a present.

Now they were back in their own part of the world. However, they refused to leave the boat. Jemmy finally explained that the people on the shore were not from his tribe. He and York were afraid of them. They were their enemies. They did not speak the same language. Jemmy's own tribe lived farther west.

The *Beagle* put out to sea again.

As the *Beagle* sailed around Cape Horn at the tip of South America, the weather turned wild again. The *Beagle* bravely fought her way through the raging sea. FitzRoy had never seen such a storm. Charles was so sick that he did not think his "spirits, temper and stomach could hold out much longer."[2] A towering wave almost tipped the boat over. Water poured into the cabin and below deck. One more wave like that, and the ship would have gone down.

They battled their way to the shelter of an

island. Charles then set about drying out the specimens in his collection.

They were now close to Jemmy's home. York came from still farther west, but he wanted to be put ashore with Jemmy and Fuegia. As the *Beagle* sailed along the coastline, smoke signals sprung up everywhere. News of the great "winged" boat was spreading fast. Crowds of Fuegians lined the beaches.

When FitzRoy spotted some flat land, he dropped anchor. This was the best place he'd seen so far for farming. Some of the crew went ashore in the rowboat. A huge crowd gathered. Everyone was screaming, "Yammer-schooner! Yammer-schooner!"[3]

It was not hard to tell what "Yammer-schooner" meant. They were all saying, "Give me! Give me!"

Jemmy felt embarrassed. He knew that the English valued good manners. He said that these people were from his tribe but not from his own family. Then his mother and brother showed up. They stared at Jemmy. He looked weird to them in his English clothes. He did not know what to say. He had no way to tell them where he had been. There weren't enough words in his language.

The sailors began to unload tools and farming supplies. They also brought ashore gifts from people in England. They had no idea what life was like in the Land of Fire. They had given Jemmy wine glasses, tablecloths, and tea trays!

For the next five days, the sailors became builders and farmers. A man named Richard Matthews was going to stay and help with the farming. He was also going to teach the Fuegians about God. The sailors built him a thatched hut. They built a storehouse for the tools. They dug the earth and planted a garden.

Every move was watched by the Fuegians.

When the work was finished, the *Beagle* went off on a short exploring trip. Matthews stood on the shore and waved. Nine days later, the ship came back. Things had not gone well. Most of the gifts had been stolen. To the Fuegians, it was really more like a game than theft. One of them would grab a piece of cloth. The others all tried to get a piece of it. In no time, it was ripped to shreds.

When the *Beagle* sailed away, Matthews was on board. He had decided not to stay after all. York, Fuegia, and Jemmy were left behind. York was taking Fuegia for a wife. They planned to go and find his tribe. Jemmy was on his own to teach English and farming. Sadly, he watched the ship leave.

The *Beagle* sailed back up the east coast of South America. There were more charts to make. A year later, she returned to the Land of Fire. Charles had heard rumors of tribal wars. As the *Beagle* drew near Jemmy's home, Charles was worried. There were no columns of smoke. Then he spotted a canoe bobbing in the water. The man in the canoe was scrubbing the paint off his face. Could this be Jemmy? It was hard to be sure. He was thin, naked, and dirty. His long hair was tangled.

The man greeted them in English. He was Jemmy all right. The captain welcomed him on board. He was given clothes to wear. FitzRoy asked him to stay for dinner. Jemmy's table manners were perfect. But he didn't eat much. The food was too rich after a diet of mussels and berries.

Things had not gone well between Jemmy and York. After the *Beagle* sailed, York built himself a big canoe. He asked Jemmy and his mother to go west with him and Fuegia. Jemmy agreed. They loaded Jemmy's gifts into the canoe. On the way west, York deserted Jemmy, leaving him with nothing.

FitzRoy asked Jemmy if he wanted to go back to England. He said, "No!" He now had a wife.

Jemmy said good-bye to the crew for the last time.

As the *Beagle* sailed away, Charles watched the smoke from Jemmy's farewell fire curl into the air. The way the Fuegians lived in this harsh land gave him a lot to think about. Everyone was equal. Yet this held them back. Until they had a chief or a government to lead them they would not become civilized.[4]

The Enchanted Isles

THE *BEAGLE* HAD NOW BEEN GONE FROM England for two and one-half years. FitzRoy had mapped the east coast of South America. He was now mapping the west coast. Progress was slow. He kept doubling back to check his charts. Also, the weather was against him. They were now sailing on the Pacific Ocean. Pacific means "peaceful," but the ocean was not living up to its name.

The slow pace gave Charles time to take trips inland. He explored the rugged country. He climbed mountains. He fought his way through forests. He collected more specimens. On one of these trips, he became very sick. He was in bed for over a month. His poor health years later may have been tied in with this illness.

On one trip ashore, Charles was lucky enough to feel an earthquake first hand. At least, he thought he was lucky! He was resting in a forest when the ground began to shake. He jumped to his feet. It was like standing on the deck of a rolling ship or skating on thin ice.

Further up the coast, Charles saw damage from the quake. In the port city Concepción, not one house was left whole. The shore was littered with broken chairs and tables and even the roofs of houses. The land around the bay had risen. Beds of rotting mussels were ten feet above the high tide mark. The shells were still clinging to the rocks. Charles recalled the band of shells high on the face of a cliff on a Cape Verde Island. So this was how the shells had gotten there. The earth had moved.

Charles had just been reading Charles Lyell's *Principles of Geology*. Lyell's book was about the forces that change the land. Charles was seeing geology happen!

One of Charles's goals was to cross the Andes Mountains. He hired a guide and ten mules. It was a hard trip, but well worth it. Again he found fossil shells. This time they were near the top of a mountain. These same shells had once been at the bottom of the sea. He collected as many as he could carry. When Charles reached the crest of the ridge, he looked back. The air was clear. The sky was deep blue. Bright-colored rocks stood out against the white snow. He wrote in his journal that it was like "hearing in full orchestra a chorus of the Messiah."[1]

At long last FitzRoy had finished his charts. They could now go home. But that was half a world away. They set out across the Pacific. Their first stop was the Galápagos Islands, where they could take on fresh water and fresh meat.[2] The meat was tortoise meat. A month later, the *Beagle* sailed with thirty giant tortoises on board.

The Galápagos are volcanic islands. Few plants grow on the black lava rock. Charles was reminded of the ironworks back home. The vents of old volcanoes looked like black smokestacks.

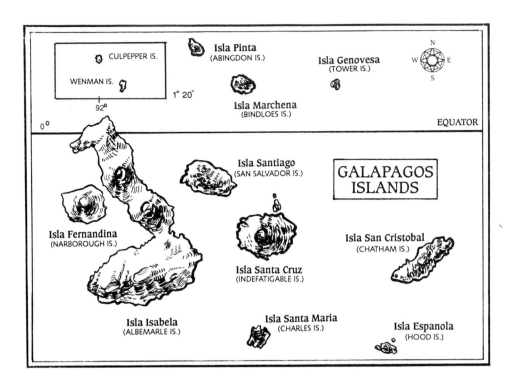

While the *Beagle* explored the channels and inlets, Charles spent a week camping on James Island (Isla Santiago). He felt as if he was living on a land that was under a magic spell. Dragon-like lizards crowded the shore. Giant tortoises plodded up a path to a freshwater spring. They drank their fill and then plodded down the path again. Charles timed the tortoises. They could walk sixty yards in ten minutes. That meant they could walk a mile in five hours. He watched one stop to eat a cactus. It stared at him and then plodded on. Another gave a deep hiss and then tucked its head into its shell.

The lizards on the shore were marine animals. They ate seaweed. They never went more than ten yards inland. But the strange thing about them was that they appeared to hate the sea. When Charles threw one into a tidal pool, it came

The Galápagos islands are a rough and forbidding landscape. They were formed by the still-active volcanoes that dot the islands.

The tortoises of the Galapágos Islands have one of the longest lifespans in the animal kingdom. Some have been known to live as long as 150 years.

straight back to shore. He threw it in again. It came ashore again. Perhaps it felt safer on shore. Enemies, such as sharks, lived in the sea. It had no enemies on shore—except people.

Charles was told that each island had its own kind of tortoise. The shape of their shells differed. The mockingbirds on each island were different as well. Charles collected specimens of mockingbirds and of other birds too. There were large flocks of small birds that were hard to tell apart. They were mostly black or dark brown. However, their beaks differed. Some had heavy beaks like a parrot. Others had thin beaks.

The plants and birds on the Galápagos Islands were similar to those in South America. Could that be where they had come from originally? But they

In the Galapágos, iguanas have adapted to life in the sea.

were not the same species as he had collected there. Why should they be similar, but different?

Charles thought back to the *Beagle*'s first stop. Cape Verde Island was also hot and dry. But the kinds of plants and animals there were not like the ones he was collecting now. They were closer to species that lived in Africa.

Charles left the enchanted islands with his mind full of questions. When he came up with answers to his questions, he was ready to write *The Origin of Species*. But that was still years away.

The *Beagle* island-hopped its way home. It put in at Cocos, a coral reef in the Indian Ocean.[3] The reef formed a ring. In the middle was a green lagoon of clear water. This type of coral island is called an atoll. Charles had seen coral on the Cape Verde Islands. Now he had a chance to take a closer look. In no time, he was waist deep in the water studying coral.

Coral reefs are formed by tiny creatures called coral polyps. Millions of them live together in a colony. Coral polyps belong to the same group as jellyfish and sea anemones. Their soft bodies are protected by cups of hard limestone. The limestone skeletons of billions of animals build up the coral reef.

Coral reefs rise only a few feet above the surface of the sea. But the coral goes down into the water to a depth of several thousand feet. People used to think that the polyps built the reefs up from the ocean floor. There was a problem with this theory. Polyps get their food from the splash of the waves. How did polyps feed on the ocean floor?

Charles had an answer. It was the mirror answer to the puzzle about the fossil shells he'd found at the top of a mountain. The fossils were on the mountain because the land had risen. Here, the land was sinking. Long ago, the ocean floor must have been higher. The coral at the bottom would then be at the surface. He pictured an island with a mountain in the middle. Colonies of coral circled the shore. As the land sank, new polyps built their shells on top of the old coral. The land kept sinking and the coral kept building. Finally the whole mountain sank into the water. All that was left was an atoll—a ring of coral with a lagoon in the middle.

Charles Darwin saw nature as the product of tiny changes that had been taking place over millions of years. Most people of his time thought that the world and everything in it had been created recently by God. They believed that nothing had changed since the creation. Charles's new way of looking at things unlocked many mysteries. But he could only share his answers with those who saw things in his new way.

Emma

THE *BEAGLE* REACHED ENGLAND ON October 2, 1836. Charles could not wait to see his father and sisters. He had no way to let them know he was coming. When he got to The Mount two days later, the hour was late. Everyone was in bed. Charles did not waken them. He slipped quietly into his room and slept till morning.

Imagine their surprise when he showed up for breakfast!

Charles had changed a lot in five years. Caroline thought he was too thin. Dr. Darwin claimed he'd learned so much while he was away that even the shape of his head was different.

Charles stayed at The Mount for only a few days. He was eager to get in touch with Professor Henslow. He wanted advice. What should he do with all the specimens he had brought back? He would need help naming them. He could not do this himself. It was a job for experts.

Henslow said Charles should go to see Charles Lyell. He might agree to look at the rocks and fossils. Charles admired Lyell. He had used his geology book while he was on the *Beagle*. Lyell said he was glad to help. This was the start of a long friendship.

John Gould was asked to name the birds. At first he said he was too busy. But when Charles showed him the drab brown and black birds from the Galápagos Islands, he grew excited. They were all finches. The number of new species surprised him. There were thirteen in all. They came from different islands.

Charles puzzled over what this meant. Long ago, finches must have reached the Galápagos Islands from South America. Could it be that they had then changed in different ways on different

The geology hammers of Charles Lyell and Charles Darwin. These two men became lifelong friends after Darwin asked Lyell to help him identify rocks and fossils he had found in South America.

islands? On one island, the beaks became thicker. On another, they became thinner. This was a disturbing idea. It suggested that species themselves could change. They were not fixed.

Charles opened up a new notebook. He called it his "B" notebook. He already had an A notebook on geology. He filled the B notebook with thoughts about why there are so many kinds of plants and animals. Soon he had C, D, and E notebooks. These notebooks were the basis of *The Origin of Species*.

Charles, however, did not spend all his time thinking about science.

He was also thinking about getting married. He was in love with his cousin Emma Wedgwood. Emma was twenty-nine, a year older than Charles. She was a smart woman. She played the piano well. She knew French, Italian, and German. She liked outdoor sports. She was very good at archery.

But Charles was not sure if marriage was the right step. So he went about making up his mind in the same way as he did everything else. He made notes! On a scrap of blue paper he jotted down two headings. One said "Marry," the other "Not Marry."

The "Marry" column won. He wanted children. He wanted a companion. He also wanted someone to look after him and his house. As it turned out, looking after Charles would be a full-time job. Charles was ill, off and on, for the rest of his life. He got sick whenever he was under

Emma Darwin, age 30.

stress. Just thinking about getting married upset his stomach and gave him a headache.

The "Not Marry" side was shorter. He liked to be free to go where he wanted. He did not care for the idea of having to visit relatives. Being married would mean less time for work. But he added to the "Marry" side that he did not want to spend his life "working, working and nothing after all."[1]

It was settled that he would ask Emma to be his wife. But would she accept? Worrying about that brought on another headache.

On November 11, 1838, Charles wrote in his journal that it was "The day of days!"[2] Emma had agreed to marry him. They set their wedding day for the end of January. They rented a house in London. Charles wanted to be near the museums. By the time he unpacked all his rocks and bones, his own house looked like a museum.

Uncle Jos gave Emma and Charles £5,000. Dr. Darwin added £10,000. This was enough money for the young couple to live on. Charles could now get on with his science. At that time, scientists had to have their own income.

Charles was writing a book about his trip around the world. The book came out in May 1839. He gave it a long title: *A Naturalist's Voyage. Journal of Researches into the Natural History and Geology of the countries visited during the voyage of H.M.S. "Beagle" round the world.* It was widely praised. But some people were upset by Charles's idea that the land had risen in some places. They did not think that the fossil shells on the cliffs proved this. They claimed the shells were left there by the flood told of in the Bible in the story of Noah saving the animals from a big flood.

Charles knew that people would be even more upset if they found out what was in his notebooks. At the thought of the uproar, he took to his bed. Emma nursed him. But she wasn't feeling well either. She was expecting a baby.

The baby—a boy—was born two days after Christmas. His proud parents named him William. Charles peered into the crib where William lay sleeping. The baby screwed up his face. He looked like one of the monkeys at the zoo. Charles opened his notebook. He made notes on what made baby William frown and smile. The new father was still a naturalist.

The next year the Darwins had another baby. This time the baby was a girl. They named her Annie. Charles adored his little daughter. When Emma was expecting her third baby, the Darwins went house-hunting. They needed a bigger house. They also wanted to get out of the city. Maybe the smoky air was making Charles sick. They found a place sixteen miles south of London. In those days, that was deep in the country. The house was named Down House. It was near the village of Downe. Mary was born a few days after the Darwins moved into Down House. She lived for only three weeks. This was a sad start to their life in their new home. But there would be more babies. Emma gave birth to ten children in all. Seven lived to be adults. In those days, people had large families.

Charles was a gentle and loving father. He liked to romp and play with his children. Each day he walked around his garden on a path called the Sandwalk. It was his thinking path. The children joined him on his walks. Sometimes they helped with his science experiments. Frank, the third son, was the best naturalist.

When the children were ill, they slept on the couch in the study while Charles worked. One time when Lenny was small, he was bouncing on the

Searching for a quiet place to live and work, Darwin and his family moved out of London to Downe. When the village changed the spelling of its name, Down House kept the old spelling.

Charles Darwin, age 30.

couch. This was not allowed. Charles said he did not want to see his son doing that. The little boy answered, "Then I advise you to go out of the room!"[3] Charles had to turn away to hide his smile. He would never have dared to talk to his own father like that!

Barnacles on the Brain

DOWN HOUSE SUITED CHARLES. HIS health improved—at least, for a while. Although he lived quietly, he was not a hermit. He kept in touch with other scientists through letters. Sometimes these scientists spent a day or two at Down House. A visit with Charles was more like an oral exam than a holiday. After breakfast he invited his guest to his study. He had a number of slips of paper on his desk. On them were things he wanted to ask them. He went through the questions one by one.

Charles's work began to pile up. He was writing a book on geology. The plants he had collected on the Galápagos Islands were still to be named. Henslow said that a young man named Joseph Hooker might name them. Hooker was a botanist. He had just come back from a four-year trip to Antarctica. He was twenty-six, eight years younger than Charles. On his trip, he had read about the

Charles Darwin's study.

voyage of the *Beagle*. He was eager to meet the author. He said he would love to look at the plants.

Almost half the plants from the Galápagos Islands were new species. Most of them were from one island. Charles went back to his notebooks. The plants fit with what Charles knew about the birds and tortoises.

In 1844 Charles wrote up all his notes on evolution. The essay was 230 pages long. It was really an outline of *The Origin of Species*. But the book itself would not be written for another fifteen years. Charles was not ready to let people know what he was thinking. It would be too stressful. Evolution was still condemned by scientists and the church. Also, Charles wanted to collect more evidence. It would take a watertight argument to convince people that species had really changed.

Charles's health was growing worse again. Sometimes he could not work for more than an hour at a stretch. His heartbeat was unsteady. During the day, he had stomach pains and vomited. At night, he could not sleep. And he had boils. Emma nursed him patiently, but it was a difficult time, especially when she was pregnant.

To this day, doctors do not know the cause of Charles's poor health. Some think his illness may have been imaginary. Or it may have been caused by something he picked up in South America.[1] It seems most likely, however, that his symptoms were brought on by stress.

His biggest worry was still what people would think about evolution. It preyed on his mind. Some days he was afraid that he might not live to finish the book. He let Emma read his essay. She found his new ideas hard to accept. But she promised to have the essay published, if Charles should die. She was to ask Lyell to edit it. Lyell did not agree with evolution of plants and animals, but he did believe in slow changes in the landscape.

By this time Joseph Hooker was Charles's closest friend. In 1844 Charles had told him in a letter that he was sure that "species are not (it is like confessing a murder) immutable."[2] He was saying that species could change. He added that he thought he had found out the simple way in which this could come about.

Only one specimen from the *Beagle* collection still needed a name. The trip around the world had lasted five years. Studying the collection had taken ten years. Charles was glad that the end was in sight. But it was really still eight years away.

The last specimen was a type of barnacle. Barnacles spend their adult lives stuck to things such as rocks. They have shells like mussels or snails. The young ones swim free. Barnacles are closer to shrimps or crabs than to shellfish.

Even for a barnacle, this one was unusual. Charles called it an "illformed little monster."[3] It lived as a parasite inside the shell of a sea snail. It was about the size of the head of a pin. Charles looked at it under his microscope. It was certainly odd. But to know how odd it was, he needed to look at other barnacles.

Charles wrote and asked his friends for barnacles. He wrote to museums. He contacted explorers. He got hold of collections of fossil barnacles. Soon his study was full of barnacles. So

Microscope of Charles Darwin.

were his thoughts. He spent hours each day peering into his microscope. When he needed a break, he walked around the Sandwalk.

A friend said that Charles had "barnacles on the brain!" One of his sons thought that everyone's father looked at barnacles. Wondering about a neighbor, he asked, "Where does he do *his* barnacles?"[4]

During the barnacle years, Charles went to several doctors. They did not know what was wrong with him. Then he heard about Dr. Gully's "water cure." He decided to give it a try, but he did not want to go away from home without Emma. And Emma could not go without the children. There were six at this time. So the whole family moved to Dr. Gully's spa for four months. Charles's health improved. Maybe this was due to the water cure. Maybe the break from writing helped. The cure itself was hard work. First Charles had to work up a sweat. Then he was drenched with icy water. He took seven-mile walks each day. When the Darwins went back to Down, Charles had a cold shower built in the garden.

In the spring of 1851, tragedy struck the Darwin family. Ten-year-old Annie was ill. Her sickness was like her father's. She had pains in her stomach, and her head hurt. Charles sent Annie to Dr. Gully's spa. He was sure that the water cure would help her. But the illness grew worse. Dr. Gully could not save Annie. Her death was a terrible grief to Charles and Emma.

When Charles was through with the barnacles, he went back to his book on evolution. But the eight long years working on barnacles had not been wasted. Charles had found that barnacles from the same species are not all alike. This was what made it hard to tell one species from another. The fact that plants or animals of the same species vary was a key to how new species come about.

Two years later, Charles had written ten chapters in his book. Then came a terrible blow. It arrived in the form of a letter. The letter was from a young naturalist in Malaysia. He was named Alfred Russel Wallace. The letter included an essay on evolution. Wallace's essay appeared to have exactly the same ideas as Charles's book. It

Alfred Russel Wallace in later years. As a young man he came up with a theory about natural selection similar to Darwin's.

was as if he had been reading Charles's mind. But Wallace was writing from the other side of the world. He asked Charles to send the essay on to Lyell if it was good.

Poor Charles! When he published his book, Wallace would think he had stolen his idea. If he did not publish it, twenty years of work would be wasted.

What should he do?

The Origin of Species

CHARLES WANTED TO DO WHAT WAS right. He wrote to Lyell and enclosed Wallace's essay. In the letter, he said, "I would far rather burn my whole book than that he or any other man should think that I behaved in a paltry spirit."[1]

Lyell already knew that Charles was working on evolution. Hooker had told him about the essay Charles had written back in 1844. Lyell asked Charles for a copy. The fair thing to do would be to read the first part of Charles's essay and then Wallace's essay at the same scientific meeting. This would show that Charles had come up with the idea first.

Charles did not go to the meeting. But the uproar he expected did not happen. Thirty-two people heard the papers. Afterwards, no one said a thing. The scientists needed time to think about these new ideas.

The evolution question was now out in the

A view of the garden where Darwin spent many quiet moments.

open. For Charles, there could be no turning back. He finished his book at top speed. It was shorter than he planned. Even so, it is almost 500 pages long.

When *The Origin of Species* was published in 1859, it was an instant success. All 1,250 copies sold out on the first day. More had to be printed.

And this time there was an uproar!

Many people were upset by this new theory of evolution.

Charles did not say that God had not created life on earth. What he said was that creation did not happen all at once. Plants and animals change over time. Species are still changing. Charles claimed that plants and animals living today are descended from similar species that lived long ago. This was supported by his studies of fossils.

Darwin's theory rests on three main points:

1. Plants and animals have more off-spring than are needed to replace the parents.

2. The overall number of each kind of plant or animal mostly stays about the same.

3. The offspring of a set of parents are not all exactly alike.

Twenty years earlier, Charles had read a book by Thomas Malthus. Malthus said that the number of people is always growing faster than the food supply. Wars, disease, and famine help to keep the numbers down.

Charles saw that what was true for people was true for other living things. Numbers are kept in check by the fight for space and by disease. Some die from lack of food. Some die when they end up as someone else's food. Darwin called this the struggle for existence.

To prove his first main point, Charles counted the seeds from a single orchid plant. There were 24,080. That was 24,078 more offspring than were needed to replace the two parents. If each of these seeds grew into a plant and if all of these plants had 24,080 seeds, the whole world would be knee-deep in orchids. But this is not the case. Some seeds are eaten by bugs. Some land on poor soil. Seedlings become sick or are crowded out by other plants. These are the losers in the struggle for existence.

This was part of the key to how new species come about. The other part was point number three. Offspring are different from their parents. All the children in one family are not exactly alike. Nor are all the orchids from the same set of parent plants exactly alike. Some are more suited than others to win out in the struggle for existence.

Charles could now explain why there were so many different species of finches on the Galápagos Islands. He could also explain why different species were found on different islands.

A long, long time ago, one kind of finch lived on the islands. But all the islands were not exactly the same. On one, insects were common. On another, the main food was seeds. Yet another had lots of cactus plants.

Long thin beaks were good for catching insects. On the island with lots of insects, finches with long thin beaks ate better than did those with short, strong beaks. When there weren't enough insects to go around, birds with long thin beaks

A.	Woodpecker Finch	D.	Mangrove Finch
B.	Warbler Finch	E.	Small Ground Finch
C.	Cactus Finch	F.	Medium Ground Finch

Darwin's theory of evolution explains why so many species of finches live on the Galápagos Islands.

Down House is now open to the public. Some tourists sit at his desk hoping to pick up some of his genius.

got more food. Because they ate better, they laid more eggs. The young birds had long thin beaks like their parents. Over time, the finches with short beaks lost out. Only long, thin-beaked finches were left on that island.

On another island, seeds were the main source of food. Strong, thick beaks were best for cracking seeds. Birds with strong beaks got the most food. More of them survived. They laid more eggs. Their offspring mostly had strong thick beaks like their parents. Some had even stronger and thicker beaks. These were the ones that ate best and had the most offspring. Over time all the finches on that island had strong thick beaks.

The same sort of thing happened on the island with lots of cactus plants. The finches that best fit the food supply survived. The survival of the fittest is what happens when the struggle for existence shapes new species.

This does not only take place on islands. It is at work everywhere.

Take giraffes, for example. Long, long ago, the ancestors of giraffes did not have very long necks.

But animals with slightly longer necks could reach leaves on higher branches. When food was scarce, they got more to eat. They had the most offspring. Their offspring had longer than average necks. The ones with short necks lost out. Long-necked animals could also see farther. They could spot predators. They could swing their heads and use their stubby horns to defend themselves. Long necks had lots of advantages.

Natural selection favored long necks. Long-necked animals survived.

Charles started his book by writing about tame animals. Dogs, horses, and pigeons are different from their wild ancestors. You could never mistake a poodle for a wolf. Poodles result from years and years of breeding. Darwin talked to animal breeders. They told him that they selected animals for parents that had the characteristics they hoped to see in the offspring. Not all the offspring were alike. The breeders saved the ones with the characteristics they wanted. These, in turn, became the parents of the next generation. Charles called this artificial selection.

Charles asked questions. But he also liked to find things out for himself. So he started his own breeding program. For years, he kept pigeons in his garden. The children took turns feeding them. Part of why Charles's book took a long time to write was that he liked to know things firsthand.

Charles also did a simple experiment to show the struggle for existence among plants. He cleared a small patch of ground. Each day he marked any new seedlings. By the end of the summer, he had counted 357. They did not all live. Only 17 percent won out in the struggle for existence. Slugs and insects got most of the seedlings.

The ideas in *The Origin of Species* are not hard to follow. But people who were hearing about evolution for the first time found them hard to accept. There are still people today who do not agree with Darwin's book.

It is too bad that Charles did not know about the work of another great scientist. This scientist was an Austrian monk named Gregor Mendel. While Charles was busy with his book, Mendel was growing peas in the abbey garden. He, too, had noticed that not all the offspring of a set of parents are the same. He mated tall and short pea plants. He mated plants with different colored flowers. He kept track of these characteristics in the offspring. He came up with three rules or laws of heredity. These laws predict what the offspring will look like.

Mendel wrote two papers on the laws of heredity. They came out in 1865 and 1869. Hardly anyone read them. It was 1900 before his work became famous. That was too late for Mendel. He died in 1884.

It was also too late for Charles Darwin.

From Apes to Worms

IN THE SPRING OF 1860, PEOPLE WERE still arguing about *The Origin of Species*. The tide was turning against Darwin. Some people agreed with parts of the book. But Charles saw everyone as being either totally for him or totally against him. His friends Hooker and Huxley were both for him. Charles was not sure about Richard Owen. Owen had named some of the fossils from the *Beagle*.

Owen was looked up to as a scientist.[1] People listened to him. Up till now, he had only hinted that species could change. Charles was eager to see if *The Origin* would win him over. It didn't.

Owen did not like Darwin's friends, especially Huxley. He acted meanly. He wrote a forty-five-page review of *The Origin*. He made fun of parts of it. The review was not signed, but Charles knew who had written it. Pages were devoted to praise for the great Professor Owen!

Charles was upset that an old friend could be so spiteful. He was more hurt than angry.

Finally, a debate took place in Oxford, when all sides had their say. Crowds of people showed up. The meeting had to be moved to a bigger hall. Professor Henslow was in charge. Henslow had given Charles the chance to sail on the *Beagle* almost thirty years earlier.

The main speaker for the older scientists and the church was Bishop Wilberforce. His critics called him Soapy Sam because he could sway an audience. He did not know much about biology. But Owen had been coaching him.

Charles did not go to the meeting. He was, as usual, sick. Even if he had been well, he was too shy to argue in public. Hooker and Huxley went to give his side. Huxley almost backed out. He thought the audience was too close-minded. At the last minute, he was talked into showing up.

Wilberforce began to speak. He belittled Charles's ideas, and the audience cheered him on. The bishop ended with a joke that played into Huxley's hands. He asked Huxley if he was descended from an ape on his grandmother's or his grandfather's side!

Huxley rose to his feet. He tried to answer the bishop point by point. He finished by saying he'd sooner have an ape for an ancestor than a man who spoke nonsense at a scientific meeting.

This was no way to talk to a bishop! The hall was in an uproar. A woman fainted and had to be carried out. Then a lean, gray-haired man stood up and waved a big black Bible. He shouted that the book in his hand held the whole truth. The gray-haired man was none other than Captain FitzRoy. He was no doubt sorry now that he had taken Charles on the *Beagle*.

Hooker then jumped into the fray. He took on the bishop, pulling apart his speech. He argued that the bishop could not have read *The Origin of Species*, his objections to evolution were so silly.

Darwin's ideas were being heard.

Hooker believed Darwin's theory. But he was fighting for another cause as well. Until then, people did not study biology as a career. Biologists were either well-off, like Darwin, or had an income from the church. Some were clergymen. Others were professors in church schools. Hooker and Huxley were the first of a new group. They were paid scientists. They were eager to draw a line between themselves and the church.

What upset people most about evolution was the idea of being related to the apes. Charles does not say this anywhere in *The Origin of Species*. But it is there between the lines, and people felt it lowered mankind. The press, on the other hand, loved it. People and apes as cousins was a gift to cartoonists. Charles, with his flowing beard and gentle face, made a fine ape.

Ten years later, Charles did take on the subject of our place in the animal kingdom. He wrote a book called *The Descent of Man*. He pointed out

Charles Darwin as an old man.

that our body structure is like that of other mammals. The last few bones of our spines are like a lost tail. A human embryo is hard to tell from the embryo of a lower animal. What sets us apart is the size of our brains. We are smarter than other animals. We are also weaker. Brains have been useful in the struggle for existence. In early times, people who could outsmart predators and prey survived. Natural selection was on the side of big brains.

To Charles's surprise, *The Descent of Man* did not cause another uproar. By now most people accepted his theory. They found that it need not destroy their belief in God. It helped explain the process of creation.

With his theories out in the open, Charles could now get on with his science. His latest passion was earthworms.

Charles always found worms interesting. Years earlier, Uncle Jos had remarked on how much soil worms could move. He and Charles were walking through a field where lime had been spread. Charles dug down into the soil. He found lime two and a half inches below the surface. Worms had been plowing the field.

The slow changes brought about by worms fit in with Charles's ideas that changes in nature are gradual. Now, on his walks around the Sandwalk, he counted worm tracks. Soon he had pots of earthworms all over his study. He spent days—and nights—watching them. The worms came to the surface at night. They dragged leaves into their holes. They also took down scraps of paper. They seemed to sense the shape of things. They always took leaves down by their stem end. They dragged a triangle of paper into the soil by its point.

Charles shone lights on his worms. Red and blue lights did not bother them. A bright clear light sent them back to their holes. Next, Charles tested their hearing. He blew a shrill whistle near the pots. The worms did not respond. He tried a bassoon. They did not respond. He took the pots through to the parlor. The worms ducked into their holes when he played the note C on the piano!

Charles also studied worms outdoors. He

made a trip to the famous stone circle at Stonehenge. Thick turf had built up around and over some of the stones that had fallen. Over the ages, worms would bury the ancient stones. He placed a large round stone in his own garden so that he could watch the worms at work. He called it the Worm Stone. It is still there. It has now been there for more than 100 years. Visitors to Down House can see one of Darwin's experiments still in progress.

Worm Stone.

Charles's first experiments were done when he was a boy with his brother Ras. He still liked doing experiments. Whenever he could, he used them to back up his ideas. But his theory of evolution could not be proved by experiments. They would take too long. When it comes to evolution, long can mean millions of years.

11

The Final Years

CHARLES'S HEALTH IMPROVED AS HE grew older. Maybe having his theory out in the open freed him from stress. Maybe the illness had run its course. He still went quietly about his science. The books he was writing now would not cause an uproar. He wrote his life story for his children. He wrote a book on earthworms. When he wasn't studying or writing letters, he liked to listen to Emma playing the piano. She read novels to him in the afternoon while he rested. Each evening they played two games of backgammon. He kept a running score of their battles. In a letter to a friend in America, he wrote, "Emma, poor creature, has won only 2,490 games, whilst I have won, Hurrah, Hurrah, 2,795 games."[1]

The children were now grown. Charles was still close to them. They visited Down House every chance they had. Frank lived at home with his son Bernard. Bernard's mother had died when he was born. Little Bernard liked to go around the Sandwalk with his grandfather. He helped his grandpa study worms.

The drawing room at Down House.

In his last years, Charles was showered with honors. Awards came from all over the globe. Charles lost count of them. In spite of the awards, he was still a humble man. When *The Origin* first came out, Charles was dismayed by people's anger. Now he was surprised by their praise. In the book he wrote about his own life, he claimed that he had only average ability. The last lines are ". . . it is truly surprising that thus I should have influenced to a considerable extent the beliefs of scientific men on some important points."[2] In the end, he was surprised that he had changed our way of seeing things.

Charles died from a heart attack in 1882. He was seventy-three years old. Emma was at his side.

His family planned to bury him in the village churchyard. Two of his baby children were buried there. So was his brother Ras. But that was not to be. The people of England wanted to honor Darwin. He was buried instead in Westminster Abbey.

Mourners came to his funeral from all over the world. His sons and daughters were there. So were

Downe Village Church. Darwin's family wanted to bury him beside his brother and two infant children. He was buried instead in Westminster Abbey.

his friends Huxley and Hooker and even Alfred Wallace. But Emma did not go. She stayed home at Down House. That was where she felt close to Charles.

Charles Darwin lies beside another great man of science, Sir Isaac Newton. It is a fitting resting place. Both these men gave the world important scientific truths.

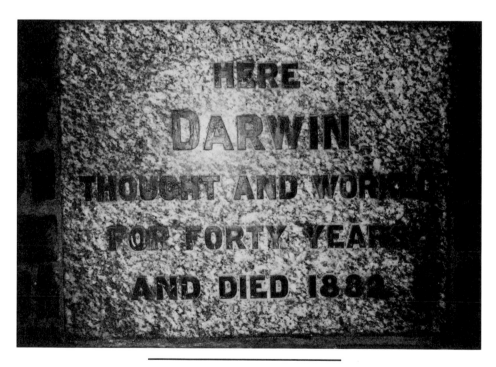

Since his death, Darwin has become one of the most well known and revered of England's great scientists.

In Darwin's Footsteps

CHARLES DARWIN WAS A VERY CURIOUS man. He was forever asking questions. He listened to the answers. He also found answers for himself. By training your mind to ask questions, you can walk in Darwin's footsteps.

Knee Deep in Dandelions

The theory of evolution is based on the fact that plants and animals have more offspring than are needed to replace the parents. You can prove that this is true for dandelions.

Find a dandelion plant that is in flower. Dandelions are hardy weeds. They grow in waste ground in cities, in parks, and in the country. They also grow in lawns. You will need a calculator, unless you are very good at multiplication. (Darwin did not use a calculator!)

Begin by counting all the flowers on your plant. Include dead flowers and buds. Now, choose a flower that has gone to seed. Pick it carefully. You don't want to lose any seeds. Carry it indoors to the kitchen table—or wherever you have set up your laboratory. Take the seeds off the head and count them. Each seed has its own parachute to carry it off in the wind. Be careful that they don't blow away.

If each seed grew into a plant, how many plants would that make? If each plant had the same number of flowers as the one you looked at, how many flowers would that make?

How many seeds could all these flowers produce?

If each of these seeds grew into a plant, and if each four plants took up a square foot of ground, how much ground would the dandelions take up? How does this relate to Darwin's theories? Think back to last year. Are there more plants now than last year? Fewer? The same?

A Fight for Life

Charles studied the struggle for existence by clearing a small patch of ground. He then kept track of what came up.

You can do this experiment too. Dig over a small area of earth in the spring or summer. If you don't have a good place to dig, you could fill a box with earth and put it outdoors. Wait for seeds to sprout. Or you can scatter seeds on the soil.

When a seedling shows up, place a toothpick beside it. This helps you keep track of the ones you've counted. Be careful not to damage the roots. How many of these seedlings grow into full-size plants? How many lose out in the struggle for existence?

Your Own Worm Zoo

Most people think of worms as blind, dumb, slimy creatures. Darwin showed they could be both smart and helpful. He improved their image. His book on worms was more popular than his book

It was along this path that Darwin did some of his most important work—thinking.

on evolution. Many of his readers wrote to him. They all had worm stories to tell.

Make yourself a worm zoo and see what you can find out about worms.

You will need a wide-mouthed jar or a small fish bowl. Fill it with topsoil. You will also need some worms. They live in good soil. Look in places where there are dead leaves.

Be careful not to let your wormery dry out. The soil should not be too wet, either. Place a few dead leaves on the top of the soil.

When are the worms active? Do they respond to noise? Try playing the piano for them like Charles did. Are they disturbed by light?

You could also make a worm stone. All you need to do is lay a flat stone on the earth and label it. As worms tunnel through the earth under the stone leaving air spaces, the stone sinks into the soil. But don't expect quick results. Worm power is very slow.

A Voyage of Discovery

Charles toured the world for five years. Later he

walked around his garden nearly every day. He called the Sandwalk his thinking path. Whether he was on his way around the world or around his garden, he was on the lookout for anything new or different. He made notes on what he saw.

You, too, can go on a voyage of discovery. Take a walk through your neighborhood, or around your yard, or around the school playground. Find out the names of the plants and animals you see. You can do this by looking them up in books at your library. Or you can ask someone. Darwin often went to other people for answers. Carry a notebook that is small enough to fit into your pocket or backpack and take notes. When you get home, rewrite them on index cards. You can then group your notes by place or by species. Use a system that works for you.

Make the same trip several times. Go at different times of the day and at different times of the year. What changes do you see? Record them in your discovery notebook.

In Darwin's time, people were great collectors. They would take samples of plants and animals for

Though the center of controversy in his lifetime, Darwin was much honored after his death. He was buried in Westminister Abbey—a place of honor.

study. Today there are more people around and fewer plants and animals. If we observe living creatures rather than collect them, then people in the future can observe them, too.

Many of the things you see on your voyage of discovery may not be new to science. What is important is if it is new to you. Learning by using all your senses is physical fitness for the mind.

Give your mind a workout!

That's what Charles Darwin did. It made him famous.

Notes by Chapter

Chapter 1

1. Dr. Erasmus Darwin's book was called *Zoonomia*.

2. Nora Barlow, ed., *The Autobiography of Charles Darwin 1809–1882* (New York: W. W. Norton, 1958).

Chapter 2

1. Nora Barlow, ed., *The Autobiography of Charles Darwin 1809–1882* (New York: W. W. Norton, 1958), p. 22.

2. Barlow, *Autobiography*, p. 22.

3. John Bowlby, *Charles Darwin* (New York: W. W. Norton, 1990), p. 58.

4. Barlow, *Autobiography*, p. 28.

Chapter 3

1. Adrian Desmond & James Moore, *Darwin* (New York: Warner Books, 1991), p. 22.

Chapter 4

1. Nora Barlow, ed., *The Autobiography of Charles Darwin 1809–1882* (New York: W. W. Norton, 1958).

2. Barlow, *Autobiography*, p. 72.

3. Charles Darwin, *A Naturalist's Voyage. Journal of Researches into the Natural History and Geology of the coun-*

tries visited during the voyage of the H.M.S. "Beagle" round the world (London: John Murray, 1888), p. 207.

4. Darwin, *A Naturalist's Voyage*, p. 12.

Chapter 5

1. Charles Darwin, *A Naturalist's Voyage* (London: John Murray, 1888), p. 205.

2. Adrian Desmond & James Moore, *Darwin* (New York: Warner Books, 1991), p. 134.

3. Darwin, *A Naturalist's Voyage*, p. 219.

4. Darwin, *A Naturalist's Voyage*, ch. 10, describes Darwin's visits to Tierra del Fuego.

Chapter 6

1. Charles Darwin, *A Naturalist's Voyage* (London: John Murray, 1888), p. 322.

2. Darwin, *A Naturalist's Voyage*, ch. 17, describes Darwin's visit to the Galápagos Islands.

3. Darwin, *A Naturalist's Voyage*, ch. 20, describes coral formations.

Chapter 7

1. Adrian Desmond & James Moore, *Darwin* (New York: Warner Books, 1991), p. 257.

2. Desmond & Moore, *Darwin*, p. 269.

3. John Bowlby, *Charles Darwin* (New York: W. W. Norton, 1990), p. 302.

Chapter 8

1. While in South America, Charles was bitten by a Benchuca bug, which is a carrier of Chagas' disease.

2. Francis Darwin, ed., *The Autobiography of Charles Darwin and Selected Letters* (New York: Dover, 1958), p. 184.

3. Adrian Desmond & James Moore, *Darwin* (New York: Warner Books, 1991), p. 339.

4. Ruth Moore, *Charles Darwin* (New York: Knopf, 1966), p. 113.

Chapter 9

1. Francis Darwin, ed., *The Autobiography of Charles Darwin and Selected Letters* (New York: Dover, 1958), p. 197.

Chapter 10

1. In 1841, Sir Richard Owen had thought up the name "dinosaur" for a new group of fossil bones.

Chapter 11

1. Ruth Moore, *Charles Darwin* (New York: Knopf, 1966), p. 190.

2. Nora Barlow, *The Autobiography of Charles Darwin 1809–1882* (New York: W. W. Norton, 1958), p. 145.

Chronology

1809—February 12: Charles was born to Susannah and Robert Darwin in Shrewsbury, England.

1817—Susannah Darwin died.

1818—Charles became a boarder at Shrewsbury School.

1825–27—Charles studied medicine at Edinburgh University, Scotland.

1828–31—Charles studied to become a minister at Cambridge University, England.

1831–36—Charles sailed around the world as a naturalist on the *Beagle*.

1839—January 29: Charles married his cousin Emma Wedgwood.

May: Publication of *A Naturalist's Voyage*.

December 27: Birth of William, the first of Emma and Charles's ten children.

1842—The Darwin family moved to Down House, Kent.

1844—Charles wrote a 230-page essay on the origin of species.

1846—Charles began his study of barnacles that would last eight years.

1848—Charles's father, Robert Darwin, died.

1851—Daughter Annie died.

1858—June: Charles received Alfred Russel Wallace's essay.

July: Wallace's paper and parts of Charles's essay on evolution were read to the Linnean Society.

1859—Publication of *The Origin of Species*.

1871—Publication of *The Descent of Man*.

1876—Charles wrote his autobiography.

1881—Publication of *The Formation of Vegetable Mold through the action of Earthworms*.

1882—April 19: Charles died at Down House. He was buried in Westminster Abbey beside Sir Isaac Newton.

Glossary

artificial selection—People who breed plants and animals decide which characteristics they want in the next generation. So the selection of which characteristics survive is artificial, not natural.

characteristic—A specific feature of an animal or plant; for example beak shape in finches, neck length in giraffes, seed size in watermelons, and eye color in humans.

evolution—The theory stating that characteristics of plants and animals change over time, eventually resulting in new species.

naturalist—A person who studies nature through observing and collecting. Naturalists keep detailed notes of their observations.

natural selection—A central part of Darwin's theory. Those members of a species who survive to breed, will pass on their genes and characteristics to the next generation. Therefore only their characteristics will continue. When the environment a species lives in changes, the characteristics needed to survive change. Only those who have the needed characteristics will survive to breed. Over time, the species may gradually change.

polyp—The name given to corals, jellyfish, sea anemones, and their relatives, when they attach themselves to a rock and no longer swim freely. They feed by using tentacles surrounding their mouth to trap food.

predator—Animals that trap or catch other animals to eat as food. A finch that eats insects, for example, is a predator.

species—A group of organisms that closely resemble one another, and are able to interbreed. Organisms that are not both from the same species cannot breed.

struggle for existence—Darwin's reasoning for why some species survive and others die out. Those members of a species best suited for living and breeding in a certain environment will survive. Those who either cannot survive, or cannot survive well, will die.

Further Reading

Bailey, Marilyn. *Evolution: Opposing Viewpoints*. San Diego, Calif.: Greenhaven, 1990.

Barnes-Svarney, Patricia L. *Fossils: Stories From Bones and Stones*. Hillside, N.J.: Enslow Publishers, Inc., 1991.

Beetles. Milwaukee, Wisc.: Raintree, 1986.

Darwin, Charles. *The Origin of Species*. Burrow, J.W., ed. New York: Viking Penguin, 1982.

Darwin, Charles. *The Voyage of the Beagle: Charles Darwin's Journal of Researches*. Brown, Janet and Michael Neve, eds. New York: Viking Penguin, 1989.

Gallant, Roy A. *Before the Sun Dies: The Story of Evoluion*. New York: Macmillan, 1989.

Margulis, Lynn. *Diversity of Life: The Five Kingdoms*. Hillside, N.J.: Enslow Publishers, Inc., 1992.

Root, Phyllis & McCormick, Maxine. *Galapagos Islands*. New York: Crestwood House, 1989.

Schafer, Susan. *The Galapagos Tortoise*. New York: Dillon, 1992.

Index